Reporting Clear

Investigating and Presenting
Your Pilot and Personal History

Cheryl A. Cage

Reporting Clear?
Cheryl A. Cage
Cover Design by Carol Core
Editing and Layout by Pam Ryan
Copyright 2000 by Cheryl A. Cage
First Printing 2000
Second Printing 2005

Printed in the United States of America
Published by ASA, Inc. 2005
Library of Congress Catalog Card Number: 00-191058

REP-CLR-2
ISBN 1-56027-509-X
     978-1-56027-509-1

DISCLAIMER: PLEASE READ
This book is sold with the understanding that the publisher and the author are not
engaged in rendering legal or medical services. The general information and advice
on gathering personal-only background information in this book is not to supersede
any specific information or advice rendered by legal or medical professionals. If legal
or medical expert assistance is required, the services of a competent professional
should be sought.
In all cases, the reader shall have final responsibility in deciding how to handle a
problem area or what information to present to a prospective pilot employer. All care
has been taken to ensure that the information contained in this book is accurate at the
time of publication. However, the reader accepts responsibility for collecting all the
information and documentation requested by the prospective pilot employer. The
reader accepts complete responsibility for the exact documentation requested by any
prospective pilot employer and they are responsible for the accuracy of the
information they provide during an interview. The publisher and author are not
responsible, in any way, for any erroneous information given to the reader by any
agency listed in this book. Use of this information does not guarantee employment or
a successful interview outcome. The author and publisher shall have neither liability
nor responsibility to any person or entity with respect to any loss or damage caused,
or alleged to be caused directly or indirectly by the information contained in this
book.
If you do not agree, or do not wish to be bound by any of the above, you may return
this book to the publisher for a full refund.

Contents

CHAPTER 1

The Importance Of Knowing

Since 1988 my professional life has been focused on aviation, primarily the professional pilot career field.

During this time I have personally worked with over 3,000 pilot-clients preparing for airline interviews and presented workshops to 5,000 more. Since expanding Cage Consulting in 1994 I have worked closely with my consultants who, conservatively, have counseled over 4,000 clients of their own.

I read about pilots and aviation. I attend, and speak at, aviation conferences. I listen to discussions and conversations led by pilot interviewers. Because of Cage Consulting's positive reputation within the aviation community I have had many pilot interviewers share their opinions and insights with me. As I learn to fly I have been rewarded with a bit of an "insider's" view of the pilot profession. My consultants and I have spent hundreds of hours debriefing clients and discussing problems, failures, and successes in order to improve our interview preparation knowledge and find better ways to teach presentation skills.

Over the years I have watched pilots struggle with all kinds of issues—some serious and some not-so-serious—but all causing worry and sleepless nights. (I am now so aware of the frailties of the human condition that I haven't heard anything in the last five years that has surprised, much less shocked, me!) While listening to these pilots discuss their mistakes, and the possible impact on their careers, I have learned many lessons about how to handle adversity, and how **not** to handle adversity.

One of the nice, and quite frankly, comfortable things I have learned is that no matter how different we are in personality there are many similarities among us. The one thing we all share is: we are human and we make mistakes. Sometimes, really stupid mistakes! (Yes, even pilots!)

Mistakes are common to the human condition. Which brings me to an important reality of the pilot profession. There are numerous public and private agencies that gather and store information concerning pilots' personal and professional background: the FAA, past employers, educational institutions, driver's license bureaus, etc. Although every precaution is taken to ensure the accuracy of those records, you can't get away from the fact that every single agency, whether public or private, is run by humans. And, as stated earlier, humans make mistakes!

The next reality we need to face is that airlines do extensive investigations into the backgrounds of their pilot applicants. While the majority of airlines begin their investigation **after** an interview, some now begin even **before** meeting an applicant.

Based on these facts:

- mistakes happen,
- many outside agencies have records on your personal and professional life,
- "to interview" and "to hire" decisions are made based on your background,

you should be beginning to see the need to **know exactly what will be discovered during your background check**. And, the need to know this information prior to an interview!

I had a client who did a complete background check prior to submitting his applications. When he received his FAA record it listed that he had failed his ATP checkride (which he hadn't!). After several weeks of phone calls, e-mails, and letters it was discovered that one particular FAA inspector had erroneously listed many of his checkride students as "failed."

What would have happened if this pilot hadn't taken the time to investigate his background? What if he'd simply trusted that every piece of information ever said or written about him was correct?

I'll tell you what most likely would have happened: He would have answered "No" to the question, "Have you failed a checkride?" Then, SURPRISE! the background check would uncover the "truth." He would have been labeled as less than honest and his whole career would have been affected because of a simple paperwork error. In reality he would have had to share some of the blame for the outcome because he'd been too busy, or thought it wasn't necessary, to check his facts!

Because of the tremendous amount of paperwork involved in the hiring process, airlines must trust the information that is gathered. They are simply not able to double- and triple-check each applicant's documents. So, if they get a document that says you failed a checkride, they most often will assume the (in this case, the FAA's) records are correct.

Even if you think there is nothing in your background that would be detrimental to your career progression, it can still be disconcerting to realize that each of your job applications will allow a potential pilot employer access to all types of records and information. What if somehow, someone has made a mistake preparing your employment record, FAA record, or training record?

What if:

- When I left my last job someone marked the box labeled "Not eligible for rehire" vs "Eligible for rehire"?
- That speeding ticket I had eight years ago pops up as occurring last year?
- Those "withdrawals" that were mistakenly listed on my college transcripts still appear?
- One of my checkrides was listed as "failed" when I never failed a checkride?
- My former employer said I was terminated and I wasn't?
- My credit report states I am a poor credit risk?
- My driving record lists a DUI and I've never had a ticket, much less a DUI, in my life!?

These are all real situations that have happened to our clients.

If you do have a problem in your history, an added bonus of investigating your own background is the acceptance of an interviewing reality: **you will** have to discuss your problem areas during your interviews! Accepting this inevitability will spur you to take the time to choose the words you want to use to explain the situation. You will also have time to practice your verbal presentation. All of these things will lead to a much more confident and professional style.

I can't begin to count the number of times clients have said to me, "I'm worried about _____." (Fill in the blank with any mistake from a failed checkride to a DUI). My reply is always, "Well, what have you discovered is said/listed/recorded?" Nine times out of ten the answer is, "I don't know."

Well, you must know. There is no excuse for any individual who says they are serious about a professional pilot career to attend an interview without full knowledge of all the facts an airline background check will produce. You must be the ultimate expert on your own personal and professional history.

Most pilots fall into one of the following categories:

Category A I am absolutely positive that there is nothing in my background that is detrimental to my career progression.

*Are you absolutely sure that **other people** have made no mistakes when recording your information?*

Category B I do have a situation in my background that causes me concern.

*Do you know exactly how this situation is listed in formal documents and how **other** people will remember and explain the situation?*

Category C I have a situation in my background that causes me concern and I know exactly what information is listed.

*Are you **fully** prepared to discuss the situation with an interviewer?*

Category D I have investigated all areas of my background that an airline will investigate.
And:
All information is correct.
Or
I have corrected mistakes made by others.
Or
I know what is listed concerning my problem areas. I can confidently and professionally discuss the situation with an interviewer.

My Goal

My goal in *Reporting Clear* is to have all pilots fit into **Category D**.

You will learn more about the Pilot Record Improvement Act of 1996 and gain a stronger understanding of why pilot interviewers radar-in on problem areas. You will be offered a do-it-yourself background check program. And, I will be sharing with you the lessons I've learned involving investigation and presentation of problem areas.

Armed with a thorough knowledge of your background and a proper perspective of your problem areas you will be able to present your mistakes from a position of confidence, not uncertainty!

Notes

CHAPTER 2

Pilot Record Improvement Act (PRIA) and Airline Specific Background Checks

*T*he first step toward learning about your background is to become completely knowledgeable about WHAT information airlines are required by law to gather and what **additional** information the airlines want to gather based on their individual corporate mandates.

Toward this end you must begin by reviewing the Pilot Record Improvement Act (PRIA) of 1996.

I have listed what I believe are the

highlights of the act. My goal is to simply give you a basic understanding of what the airlines face in terms of requirements for information gathering. I recommend you fully inform yourself of the specifics of this act. To do so, go to www.faa.gov. Under Search, type: pilot records improvement act. Here you should find FAQs and in-depth information concerning PRIA.

If necessary, have the intricacies of the act explained to you by a legal professional well-versed in aviation law.

Pilot Record Improvement Act Of 1996.

The Pilot Record Improvement Act of 1996 (PRIA) enhances aviation safety by enabling air carriers to make better-informed decisions when hiring pilots.

This Act provides that before hiring an applicant as a pilot, carriers must request and receive records from any carrier, company, organization, or person who has employed the applicant as a pilot during the past five years.

The records covered by the Act include:

- Federal Aviation Administration mandated alcohol and drug testing program results.
- Training, qualification, proficiency, or professional competency of the pilot, including evaluations made by a check airman.
- Any disciplinary action that was not subsequently overturned.
- Any release from employment or resignation, termination or disqualification with respect to employment.

In general before hiring an individual as a pilot, an air carrier shall request and receive the following information:

FAA Records From the Administrator of the Federal Aviation Administration, records pertaining to the individual that are maintained by the Administrator concerning:

- current airman certificates (including airman medical certificates) and associated type ratings, including any limitations to those certificates and ratings; and
- summaries of legal enforcement actions resulting in a finding by the Administrator of a violation of this title or a regulation prescribed or order issued under this title that was not subsequently overturned.

Air Carrier and Other Records From any air carrier or other person that has employed the individual **as a pilot** during the five-year period preceding the date of the employment application of the individual, or from the trustee in bankruptcy for such air carrier or person:

- Records pertaining to the individual that are maintained by an air carrier (other than records relating to flight time, duty time, or rest time) under regulations sent forth.

- Other records pertaining to the individual that are maintained by the air carrier or person concerning:
  —the training, qualifications, proficiency, or professional competence of the individual, including comments and evaluations made by a check airman,

  —any disciplinary action taken with respect to the individual that was not subsequently overturned; and,

  —any release from employment or resignation, termination, or disqualification with respect to employment.

National Driver Register Records From the chief driver licensing official of a State, information concerning the motor vehicle driving record of the individual.

Miscellaneous Before releasing the requested records, the carrier, company, organization and/or person of whom they were requested must obtain written consent of the pilot, and, if requested by the pilot, provide the pilot with a copy of such records.

The information requested must be furnished to the requesting airline not later than 30 days after receiving the request.

The carrier, company, organization and/or person providing the records is immune from federal, state, or local lawsuits brought by the pilot whose records are requested unless the information provided was known to be false by the person providing it and was maintained in violation of a criminal statue of the United States.

Airline Specific Background Checks

As you read the small print on your airline applications you will see that you are giving permission for the airline to review extensive areas of your background.

The information required by the PRIA is the **minimum** that airlines are required to collect. In addition to gathering the records required by PRIA, most airlines also do their own background checks which can include credit checks, all past employer references (not just five years), extensive driving record reviews, and perhaps even a criminal background check.

When you sign your application you are stating that everything you have listed on your application is true. Airlines take this statement very seriously. Airlines do not ask questions such as, "Have you ever had an FAA violation (moving violation, job termination, etc.) **that we can uncover**?" Many times the questions will have no time limit: "Have you **ever** (had a speeding ticket, etc.)? It is possible to overcome a serious problem in your background but it is almost impossible to overcome the appearance of being less than truthful.

An Important Note

A great deal of time was spent ensuring that listings for addresses, phone numbers, and websites were accurate. However, as we are all well aware, in this revolution of the computer things change quickly. I encourage you to visit the listed websites for the various departments to ensure that specific contact information is still current.

Please contact me with any changes or errors you may discover. My email is cheryl@cageconsulting.com or you may call toll free at 1-888-899-CAGE. Thank you!

CHAPTER 3

Do-It-Yourself Background Check

Before we begin...

You may feel as though some of the sections in this do-it-yourself background check do not apply to you. However, you **must** ensure that someone else hasn't made an error in recording your information. To be thorough, I encourage you to complete all of the following steps in order to leave no possibility for error.

Receiving a job offer, or actually being in training, does not mean that the background check has been completed. Although the PRIA has been expanded to allow airlines the time needed to collect all the required documentation, the background check must be completed prior to actually putting a new pilot employee on the line. But, it is not uncommon for a pilot to be in the last week of training and have the background check still be ongoing. You must realize that it can take as many as eight weeks to receive information from prior employers, the FAA, and the NDR. If a mistake is discovered it could take you many months to get the situation resolved.

For these reasons it is imperative that you begin your background check as soon as possible.

Don't be lulled into a false sense of security If you have a problem area that does not show up in your background check please do not assume that it will not be discovered. Many times problem areas are discovered through other than administrative channels.

Bob decided not to inform the interviewer that he was terminated from a short-lived flight instructor job. However, several of his friends know about the termination. One of these friends says (innocently) to an acquaintance, "Yeah, Bob was worried that being fired from his flight instructing would hurt him in the interview." Guess what? That acquaintance sits on the hiring board of the airline that just hired Bob!

Think the odds of this occurring is low? I am personally aware of 12 pilots who have been pulled from new-hire class because of just such situations.

A word about notarized letters I talk about the need, at various times, to have a document or letter notarized. It is important to remember that the only person who can get a letter notarized is the **person writing the letter**. For example if an airline requires a notarized letter from an individual stating your whereabouts during a period of unemployment the person writing about your whereabouts will have to personally have the letter notarized.

1. Driving Record: State And National

If you have had various driver's licenses, get records from each state where you have been licensed.

State Driving Record For most states you may request your record in person, by mail, or via the Internet. Find the location of your local Motor Vehicle Department listed in the Government section of the phone book under "Motor Vehicles." To find your state's DMV on the web, go to google.com and type in [your state] DMV. Ex: Arizona DMV

In person: Visit the Division of Motor Vehicles in the state from which you are requesting a driving record. Tell them you would like to obtain a copy of your driving record for the period of time requested by the air carrier.

Via mail: Requirements for each state vary but for most states (using Colorado as an example) the following information must be included with your request by mail:

- Your name,
- Date-of-birth,
- Driver's license number,

- Return address, and
- Check or money order for the fee charged by that particular state (in the state of Colorado the fee is $2.20)

Via the Internet:
http://www.4safedrivers.com

The price for this service runs around $20.00.

Many states have their own website which allows you to request your driving record directly from them. For addresses and phone numbers there is a comprehensive listing of DMVs for all 50 states at the National Highway Traffic Safety Administration at http://www. nhtsa.dot.gov/people/perform/driver/.

The length of time for which each state maintains driving records varies (the state of Colorado maintains driving records for only seven years).

If your state does not maintain driving records for the entire period for which the air carrier is requesting, then request the Division of Motor Vehicles to state, in writing and on state letterhead (if possible), that their records are kept for only ___ years.

REALITY CHECK! *You must obtain a driver's license in most states within 30 days of residency in that state unless you hold a military driver's license at the time. If you have not complied with this law you may be required to explain your negligence during the interview.*

REALITY CHECK! *Do not make the mistake of believing that because you received a ticket in Montana that it will not show up on your Virginia driver's license. It is important to be honest with* *yourself as you fill out applications. Airlines do not ask questions such as "How many speeding tickets have you had in the last ten years **that we can find**?" No, the question is, "How many speeding tickets have you had in the last ten years?"*

National Driving Record (NDR)   The NDR is an index of individuals who have had their driving privileges suspended or revoked for cause (DWI, suspension of license for any reason). Individual traffic violations will not necessarily show up on the NDR unless they have resulted in a penalty like the ones listed previously.

You may obtain your national driving record by sending a notarized letter which states that you are requesting a copy of your National Driving Record. Included in the letter you need to provide the following information:

- Full legal name,
- Date-of-birth,
- State of your current driver's license,
- Your Description: height, weight, sex, eye color (or you may simply make a *clear* copy of your driver's license and attach it to the letter.)

There is no charge and you should receive the NDR in approximately 10 business days. Send the letter to:

National Highway Traffic Safety Administration

400 Seventh Street SW - Room 6124A

Washington, DC 20590

Phone: 202-366-4800

www.nhtsa.dot.gov

The NDR needs the notarized letter with the above information so please do not request special attention by phone or fax.

If there is a discrepancy on your national driving record, speak with the Division of Motor Vehicles in the state in which the discrepancy occurred. **DO NOT call the National Highway Traffic Safety Administration** regarding the discrepancy as they will have no information and will refer you back to the Division of Motor Vehicles in the state in which the discrepancy occurred.

*REALITY CHECK! If you have had a DUI or a suspended license and it does not show up on the NDR do not assume that you are off the hook. If there is **one** scrap of official paper that lists your driving problems you must assume that someone, somewhere, by asking the right questions to the right person, will be able to discover the information. It could easily show up through a state license, or perhaps show up when the **airline** requests your NDR.*

REALITY CHECK! I have had some people tell me that the DUI (or speeding tickets, etc.) is no longer listed on their driving record. I then ask them if they disclosed this information on their FAA Medical. Their mouths drop open and they respond, "Oh, wow. I completely forgot about that!" Never forget that some information may be listed in several different places!

2. FAA Records

There are two ways to get copies of your airmen certification records.

1) You can request via mail. To do so you must send a signed, written request. This request must include:

- Name
- Date of Birth
- Social Security OR Certificate Number

In your letter, state "I am requesting a copy of my complete FAA Airman file for a job interview." This information will help ensure a more expeditious response.

Mail all your requests to:

Regular mail: *Federal Aviation Administration*

Airman Certification Branch, AFS-760

P.O. Box 25082

Oklahoma City, OK 73125-0082

Once the FAA receives your request *they will notify* you of fees and payment options.

2) You can also release copies of your airman certification records to a third party. To do this, visit this website and follow the directions.

via the Internet: http://www.faa.gov/licenses_certificates/ airmen_certification/

(If this website doesn't connect, go directly to the FAA home page at faa.gov and search "Airman Certification Records.")

If you send a third party your records I strongly suggest that you ALSO request your own copies.

Additional Information You May Require:

- To obtain a duplicate medical certificate or copies of your medical records, call the FAA Aeromedical Service Division at 405-954-4821,

- To speak with an FAA inspector concerning any accidents/incidents/violations, call 405-954-4173,

- To request a duplicate of licenses, call 405-954-3261 or toll-free 866-878-2498.

If you have had an FAA accident/incident/violation **and the incident has been finalized** it will be important to take documentation concerning the accident/incident/violation to your interview. (See Chapter 5 for details)

If you have an unresolved FAA accident/incident/violation please see Chapter 5 for advice.

There is a lot of good information on the FAA website at www.faa.gov.

3. Past Employment Information

Civilian Many air carriers require employment information for at least the past 10 years and in some cases for the entire period of time since high school.

You **will be** required to provide current addresses/phone numbers for those companies by whom you have been employed.

You **will be** required to include all employers and not just aviation-related employers.

***Still-in-business* past employers** Make sure that you gather the correct address, phone numbers, and fax numbers for each company. Call your previous employers and verify this information.

If the company is still in business but under new ownership or a new name make sure you highlight that fact to the airline. List the information as such: ABC Airlines (formerly DEF Airlines)

Make sure that the new management has your past employment information on file and will be able to respond in a timely manner to your potential employer requests. To do this call the Human Resources or Personnel Department of the company and speak to whoever handles "Employer Recommendations" or the person in charge of "Employee Verifications." Let your past employers know they may be receiving requests for your information.

Out-of-business past employers If you were employed by a company which is no longer in business, you will **still be required** to provide proof that you worked there. Many airlines will accept:

- A notarized letter written by a former supervisor or a co-worker which states their knowledge of your employment at that company during the period of time indicated on your application/resume, or

- A W-2 form from that employer.

To obtain W-2 forms for past employers request Form 4506 in any of the following ways:

Via Telephone: (800) 829-3676

Via Fax: (703) 368-9694 (then choose the 'tax forms' option; your fax order number is 41721)

Via Internet: http://www.IRS.gov, in the boxes on the left-hand side of the page, *search* Form 4506, *within* Forms and Publications.

In Person: You may visit your local IRS office and obtain form 4506.

It will take approximately 6 weeks to receive your W-2 forms. You most likely will be unable to obtain W-2 forms for periods of employment more than eight years ago.

Other ways of proving employment

- Company training records
- Company flight training records
- Employer critiques or evaluations.

REALITY CHECK! Aviation is an extremely small world. Perhaps you were terminated from a job. However, your past employer told you that he will say you "resigned." And, you feel secure that the fact that you had another job immediately after your "resignation" will hide the "resignation" from the interviewer. But, ask yourself: How many people know you were, in fact, terminated from this job? If it is one or more you have just increased the odds of your termination being discovered through the aviation grapevine.

REALITY CHECK! There is a person who relies on the phone numbers, fax numbers and addresses you have provided in order to complete your background check. If you are too lazy to gather the numbers or think it's ok to give a number that simply rings through to a friend of yours in the company, you are adding a great deal of work to this person's day. And you will not be gaining a friend. Remember, word gets around!

*REALITY CHECK! Review the **airline's requirements** for acceptable employment verification documentation.*

4. Employer Training Records

Civilian Airlines are interested not only in your FAA checkrides but also company training.

For airline specific training records (proficiency checks, upgrade training, etc.) as a general rule airlines must ask for and receive these records through their own channels. Do not make the assumption that if you provide your training records during the interview that they will not request the identical records on their own. However, it is important to review your records prior to any interview in case there are any errors.

Although the Pilot Record Improvement Act allows you to receive a copy of any training record that an airline requests, do not wait to review your records this way. You will be receiving the records at the same time the airline is and you will have little or no time to correct any errors.

Each state has a different set of rules concerning how an employee may review their employment records. Contact your past employers' Human Resources or Personnel Department for information on how to review your employee records.

Military

Specific Duty Stations You will be required to provide current addresses and phone numbers for each military squadron in which you served.

It is not uncommon to have a squadron no longer be in existence, but you will still be required to provide the necessary information. Normally a current phone number for your commander or a coworker who served in that particular squadron during that period of time will suffice. Go the extra mile and get a notarized letter from one of these individuals stating that you were in that squadron during that time.

A good website that might aid in your search for military addresses is www.globemaster.de

Civilian jobs during military service If you have held a civilian job during your military service you must include that information also. (See Past Employer Information–Civilian.)

Military Records At the present time military records are not easily obtained by an airline. However, you may be asked to sign a release that allows review of your military records.

Do not become complacent in thinking that your military career is going to be an "unknown." Remember that the fact that you were brought in front of a Captain's Mast, or that you were taken off flying status for whatever reason, is known to your friends and acquaintances and (sometimes!) people who don't like you very much. And, people do talk!

REALITY CHECK! Yes, it will take a lot of legwork in order to obtain the squadron information. IF YOU DO NOT OBTAIN THIS INFORMATION the message you send to the interviewers is that you expect them to do the legwork for you. This translates into a low motivation for the job. And, guess what? The company with whom you are interviewing most certainly will not do the legwork required to obtain the information! Without the information, no job!

Residency Information Many airlines are now requesting past home addresses. Although the time frame may vary (five years to since high school) it is important that you provide each address with no gaps.

To refresh your memory review old

W-2s from past jobs, college transcripts or old checking account statements or bills. If your parents, a sibling or a close friend keeps an address book you might be able to find specific addresses in their old books. If you keep old letters review the address on the envelopes.

If you have had the same doctor for a while (family or FAA) they may be able to provide you with your past addresses from their records.

5. Educational Records

College Transcripts/
Educational Records To obtain official transcripts, call the Bursar's Office at each college/university in which you were enrolled and follow their instructions. In many cases, you will be required to submit a written request including the following information:

- Student name,
- Address,
- Social Security Number,
- Number of transcripts desired,
- Signature.

Request at least 2 (two) transcripts in order to have a transcript for the air carrier and a transcript for yourself.

Don't forget to ask if there are any fees involved.

Most air carriers require certified transcripts, which, depending upon the institution, could include the following:

- Transcripts which are stamped with an official, embossed seal,

or

- Transcripts which are contained in a sealed envelope, with the seal being stamped with an official stamp. IMPORTANT: if the envelope has been opened in this case, the transcripts are no longer considered certified and official.

You will be required to **obtain an official transcript for every college/ university** in which you have been enrolled.

*REALITY CHECK! Most airlines will want transcripts from **every** college you attended (even if you only took one class). Taking your final transcripts from the college where you received your degree which lists transferred credits is NOT enough. The airline will want original transcripts from every college you attended.*

GED   A GED is considered equivalent to a high school diploma. If asked for proof of a high school diploma, your GED is that proof.

6. Passport Information

New/Replacement   You may obtain a **new *or* replacement passport in person only**. Many local post offices are able to process your application at their facility. It may require several months for the process to be completed. Call or stop-by your local post office to determine whether or not they can process your application.

Renew You may renew your passport by mail by obtaining a Form DSP-82. To download go to the U.S. Department of State website at:

http://travel.state.gov/passport/get/renew/renew_833.html

Make sure you follow the directions exactly!

If you need your passport in a hurry there is an expedited service. Go to the above website and click on "Expedited Service" in the body of the text about passport renewal. Be aware there are hefty additional fees for this service.

To find a passport agency near you go to:

http://www.travel.state.gov

Click on "Passport."
Click on "Passport Agencies."

7. Social Security Card

U.S. citizen To obtain a **replacement** Social Security card you must provide a valid driver's license at your local Social Security office and complete a request form. You should not be charged a fee. You should receive your replacement card within 2-3 weeks (but remember to plan for double that amount of time to be on the safe side!).

If you were born in the U.S. (or if you were born outside the U.S. of American citizen parents) but have resided outside the U.S. and have **never before had** a Social Security number go to your local Social Security office. You will need to provide school and/or medical records from the country in which you have been residing as well as your U.S. birth certificate and complete a request form. You should receive your card within 2-3 weeks.

Not a U.S. citizen To obtain a new Social Security card if you are not a U.S. citizen, you may go to your local Social Security office, show your green card or your passport with an I-94, and complete a request form. You should receive your card within 2-3 weeks.

To obtain a new Social Security

card if you have never before had a Social Security number and were born outside the U.S., you may go to your local Social Security office, provide proof of your INS employment authorization and visa, and complete a request form. You should receive your card within 2-3 weeks.

8. Foreign Education

If you went to school outside the U.S. it is a good idea to translate your education into U.S. terms. For information on Foreign Educational Credential Evaluation call World Education Services at:

NY office: 1-800-937-3895

Southeast Office (Miami) : 1-800-937-3899

www.wes.org.

REALITY CHECK*! It is sometimes very difficult to translate foreign education into the U.S. equivalent. If you don't go to the trouble to translate the documents ahead of time you could end up spending a lot of time explaining the course work. This leaves you less time for talking about other important facets of your background. In addition having your education translated signals that you are highly motivated.*

9. Immigration Records

You must possess and provide to the air carrier documentation that establishes both identity and employment eligibility within the United States. Each airline will have a list of what documents satisfies these requirements. However, here are some examples of what appear to be good documents:

To Establish Identity: • Driver's license,

- Voter's registration card,
- U.S. military identification.

***To Establish Employment
Eligibility:***

- Social Security card,
- U.S. Citizen ID Card,
- Unexpired employment authorization document issued by the INS.

10. Credit Report

Although not all airlines include a credit check in their background check it's included here because this is an area where mistakes are regularly made. One client's sibling had stolen his Social Security number and used it to obtain credit cards. The result was my client had several bad check charges listed under his name. It took many months to clear up this confusion.

The easiest route is to contact one of the three major credit bureaus listed below and request a credit report.

Via Telephone:

Equifax   (800) 685-1111

Experian   (800) 682-7654

TransUnion (TRW)(800) 916-8800

11. Bankruptcy

To obtain records about a bankruptcy, call the U.S. Bankruptcy Court in the state in which it was filed. Ask for bankruptcy records from the year in which it was filed. Each state varies according to local law but many times your records will already be archived, in which case they will refer you to another number.

If you have ever filed for bankruptcy, assume it is recorded! In researching this information I learned that someone had requested bankruptcy records from 1930—and was able to receive them!

12. Special Medical Situations

If you have any concerns surrounding an illness/injury/other medical condition it is important to gather all your medical records (including x-rays, if applicable) pertaining to the condition as well as a letter from your attending doctor giving you a current, clean bill of health.

If the condition occurred many years ago, it would be ideal to bring a letter stating that it has not been a problem since that time.

Medical situations will most likely not be discussed during the interview. The medical paperwork you will want to present will not be submitted at the time of the interview, but instead will be submitted during the medical evaluation.

13. Criminal Report

The possibility of an error being made in this area is small. However, to be complete I have included the information.

State Offense Because it is impossible to research every state's requirements for conducting a records search I will share with you what I have discovered is true in Colorado. However, this information will give you a good starting point no matter what state you live in.

To obtain records pertaining to any state (non-federal) offense you should contact the District Court in the county the violation occurred. Because there are many different departments within the District Court, a good place to start is with the Clerk of the Court for that county. The Clerk of the Court carries records on any type of county or district case.

If you request your records in person you may not be charged.

If you request the records search by mail it will most likely cost you a fee (in Colorado it is $5.00). Write a letter requesting any and all records pertaining to:
- Your Name,
- Date-of-birth,
- Social Security number.

Be sure to include a stamped, self-addressed business sized envelope with your request.

REALITY CHECK! Do NOT assume that the air carrier will not discover a non-federal offense. The aviation community is a very small world. The chief pilot at your desired air carrier could just be the spouse of the officer who arrested you! (I have heard stories much stranger than this!)

Federal Offense   To obtain the records pertaining to any federal offense in which you may have been involved, call the U.S. District Court in the state in which the violation occurred. Ask them for the record under your name (most states are able to perform a global search using your last name and first initial).

Each state varies as to their methods of record-keeping but the state of Colorado has computerized records back to January, 1993, and a card file system containing records back to the early 1900s!

Online you will discover many companies which will do a criminal background check for a fee. Using a major name search engine (Yahoo, Excite, Lycos, etc) and some of the following keywords: background checks, background investigations should connect you with many of these companies.

Final Reminder: Keep copies of all documents including applications, letters of recommendation, etc.!

Notes

CHAPTER 4

Tried and True Methods

Because of the results of deregulation (airline bankruptcies and massive furloughs) airline interviewers found themselves interviewing a new type of pilot applicant: experienced pilots in their 30s, 40s, and even 50s. None of these applicants were novices and many had been in aviation over 20 years!

These more mature pilots had many successes to their credit. But, because they had been in the pilot profession for awhile, many had also made mistakes. Interviewing these pilots interviewers quickly realized that although it was important to review mistakes, it was equally important to review the individual's response to a mistake. Does he accept responsibility? Does she make the same mistakes over and over, or, did she learn a lesson from the first mistake?

In addition to the **what** and **why** of the mistake, the interviewer wants to know HOW the applicant responded during and after the mistake.

Over the years I have learned a great deal about the differences between a successful applicant and an unsuccessful one. I have seen which approaches can make a problem area more of a "non-issue" and what tactics can make it a larger issue than is actually warranted.

Making sure the odds are on your side is not complicated. There is no secret method, there are no perfect words to use. Ensuring a better chance for success simply involves being honest, being prepared, and being open toward the interviewer.

Let's review various approaches exhibited by successful applicants and along the way dispel some common misconceptions about presenting problems in an interview.

A successful applicant—

Accepts responsibility I had one client who had failed his initial Captain Upgrade.

Prior to meeting with him I was not overly concerned about this one failure. He had done well in all the rest of his training, his driving record was clean, and his grades in college were above average. Although I knew that, as always, failed checkrides would be a topic of discussion I wasn't concerned that it was a major problem.

Three minutes into our discussion I realized that this individual was going to make the checkride a very major problem! He blamed his flying schedule for not allowing him time to study. He blamed the check airman for the types of questions asked during the oral. He blamed everyone but himself.

After listening to his complaints for a few moments I asked him some basic questions:

—Did someone tell you that certain areas *wouldn't* be covered? (His complaint was that he'd been asked "unfair" questions even though they were airplane specific.)

—Did you think all emergency procedures wouldn't be covered? (His complaint was that he had been given multiple emergencies.)

—Were you caught unaware as to when your checkride would be given? (His complaint was he was flying over 70 hours a month and didn't have enough time to study.)

Having a stranger bluntly ask him these questions, his demeanor changed. "I guess there was a great deal more I could have done to not have failed. All those questions you asked were valid. I did have control over the way I approached the checkride." It took us 30 minutes but he finally realized the failure was no one's fault but his own.

Although thoroughly irritated at the beginning of our conversation this client was a smart man. He was able to take the constructive criticism and effect some changes. Taking his new attitude into his interview he reported that the interviewer spent perhaps five minutes on the failure, and then moved on. He was hired.

When we are honest with ourselves we quickly recognize that our behavior almost always plays a part in contributing to our mistakes. It isn't just bad luck, or being at the wrong place at the wrong time, or being made a scapegoat. More often than not mistakes are a result of personal decisions.

Is able to spot "confident incompetents" In many areas of my life I am highly competent. However, in other areas I am, to use a term I've coined, a "confident incompetent."

I am responsible for more of my friends getting lost than any other person in the world. When I am fulfilling the role of navigator I sound extremely sure of myself. Because of my confidence, no matter how many times I've been wrong, my advice continues to be taken.

ME (forcefully): "I'm telling you, take this next right! Yes, I'm positive!"

Uncomfortable pause with companion glaring as it becomes obvious we made the wrong turn.

ME: "Oh. Hmm. This doesn't look right now does it?"

Pilots are a confident breed. Unfortunately, sometimes the confidence that is needed to fly safely spills over into areas that the pilot knows nothing about! Nowhere is this more apparent than when pilots talk about interviewing.

When deciding how to handle problem areas (actually in **any** interviewing situation) you must make sure you ask the **right** person for advice! Just as you wouldn't ask me how to do a crosswind landing, you shouldn't ask a line pilot for advice on how to discuss a problem during an interview.

One client received advice from a very experienced management captain to not inform the interviewer of his past traffic history (Wrong! See the section on driving records). Another client had a friend guarantee him that telling a joke at the beginning of the interview would set a comfortable tone (also wrong).

It is important to debrief your friends, and those acquaintances within aviation, but take their advice and suggestions with a healthy dose of skepticism.

Believes that "honesty is the best policy" Many of you might be thinking to yourselves, "I heard about a guy/ I have a friend who got away with not telling about a failed checkride/speeding tickets/job termination, etc."

Yes, there are people who were less than honest during an interview who were hired. But, there are many, many more people who get **caught** stretching or inventing the "truth."

I had one client who chose not to tell an airline interviewer about a non-flying job termination that had occurred just out of college. Because the job was not in aviation he talked himself into thinking it wasn't important to discuss during an interview.

He was successful in the interview. However, during the background check the job termination was discovered. This individual was pulled from training class and invited to the chief pilot's office.

He was asked if the termination was correct. He said "yes." He was not given an opportunity to explain the situation further and was terminated. At this point the airline's main concern was not the original termination (in fact, had he discussed it openly and honestly during the interview it most likely would have been a non-issue). The issue was now the applicant's integrity. This applicant had made a major issue out of a situation that warranted a simple five minute discussion.

Aviation is too small a world, the legalities of hiring a pilot are too specific, the possibilities of "confidential information" becoming public are too great, and the interviewing ability of today's pilot interviewer is too good to try to hide a problem area.

Puts into play lessons learned from past mistakes If an interviewer is comfortable that an applicant acts on lessons learned from past mistakes, the usual approach is to end the questioning sooner rather than later (which will allow more time to talk about good things!).

On the other hand, when a problem area is introduced and the interviewer is greeted with excuses and reasons why it "wasn't really my fault" the outcome could be very different. The applicant could face more intense questioning concerning not only the specific problem, but also about other minor problems in the applicant's background.

*Applicant: I **only** have two speeding tickets in the last two years.*

Interviewer: Tell me about them.

A: Well, I received them both on the same highway. It's common knowledge that this area is a speed trap.

I (to himself): Hmmm, he must really think rules aren't for him especially when he knows there is a speed trap and yet he still speeds!

The interviewer would then make a note to dig deeply into other areas of the applicant's life to discover if not taking responsibility and ignoring basic rules is a trend in his personality.

Faces problems head on One of the main reasons applicants get into trouble when asked to discuss a problem is that they still are sensitive about the problem. To alleviate becoming defensive you must desensitize yourself about your problems. To do this you must:

Quit ignoring the situation. Too many applicants think, "If I ignore it, it will go away." It won't. It *will* be asked about in the interview. Accept it.

Look at the situation from all sides. What actions did you take that caused this problem? Has the problem affected other parts of your life or other people? Has the problem had an impact on your career?

Make yourself accept the consequences of the problem. Quit making excuses. Quit feeling sorry for yourself. Accept responsibility for the mistake. Write down the lessons you have learned.

Verbalize your explanation of the problem to a trusted friend. How do you sound? Are you defensive, irritated? Or, does your friend feel as though you have accepted responsibility and learned some lessons? If not, you have more self-evaluation to do!

I had one client who had received a job critique which mentioned he had a tendency to be abrasive. Initially, he disagreed. However, somewhere inside himself he must have known he had this tendency.

A couple weeks after our first discussion he called me. "I think I see why people call me abrasive."

To gain some flight time he had rented an airplane with another pilot. He had also taken his wife on the flight. My client was PIC and the other pilot didn't respond quickly enough to his request to call the tower.

My client's wife told him later that she had been surprised at his abrasiveness. "I guess I'm different in the airplane. I feel it's so important to do things in a timely fashion."

We came to the conclusion that, especially when flying with someone for the first time, he should do a formal briefing just to alleviate confusion about duties. Through his openness he was able to discover the source of the reason for the criticism that he was abrasive and he found ways to deal with this shortcoming.

Presents the appropriate paperwork Whether you must discuss a violation or a misplaced logbook, offering paperwork which documents the circumstances (i.e., FAA violation finding letter, W-2s to recreate flight time) will help lower the interviewer's concern. Appropriate documentation says, "I knew you would be concerned about this problem. For this reason I have done everything possible to help you understand the situation. I am ready, willing, and able to discuss this area with you."

IMPORTANT NOTE: *Do not misread this as "inundate the interviewer with paperwork." More about this in Chapter 6*

Prepares for the entire interview I did a Special Concerns consultation with a client who had an FAA violation. This client kept saying to me, "I know I will do well in the rest of the interview if I just can become comfortable talking about the violation." After we discussed the presentation of the violation he chose not to do any other interview preparation.

Several weeks later he called with sad news. "The discussion of the violation went like a breeze. But, I was completely unprepared for the rest of the interview. I did just what you cautioned me not to do. I focused only on my problem area and forgot about the rest of my career."

Don't prepare for your problem areas alone! Remember, you could have an hour or more with an interviewer. If your problem area discussion is organized, the interviewer may only spend a few moments on it. You are then faced with a lot of time to discuss other things, both personal and technical. You must be organized and prepared for these questions also!

You are much more than this one problem! Maybe you have made some mistakes in your life, but I can guarantee you have had more successes than failures. Hey, the pilot profession is extremely competitive and you have the qualifications to compete! You should be extremely proud of this accomplishment alone!

CHAPTER 5

I've Got a Problem—Specific Suggestions and Explanations

*I*n this chapter we will discuss **why** the interviewer is so interested in any problem areas. I'll offer suggestions and explanations on the presentation of problem areas.

Please note: *Addendums are discussed in Chapter 6.*

Trends

In terms of problem areas, interviewers are looking for answers to two separate questions:

1) Why did the specific problem occur?

2) Is there a trend toward negative behavior?

Many pilots are surprised by what might be considered problem areas. Some pilots take a lackadaisical approach to interviews because they have (what appears to them) no glaring problems in their background such as: consistent training problems, DUI, suspended license, suspension from college, job termination or suspension. These pilots do not realize that some seemingly innocuous areas can be cause for concern.

Let's look at an applicant whose background, on the surface appears without noticeable problems, but in fact might cause some concern for an interviewer.

Bill is 32 years old. He earned mediocre grades in college and failed his private and CFI checkride. While working for a commuter carrier he needed additional training when upgrading to captain. Bill received two speeding tickets within the last three years.

Each or these shortcomings, taken alone, would not be cause for great concern. However, add them all together and an interviewer may begin to see a trend toward lack of motivation (poor grades, failed upgrade). The two speeding tickets might show an inability to follow rules.

Part of your interview preparation must include looking for areas that could point to a negative trend in your behavior.

If you spot a negative trend the next step is become aware of how you have improved, or look for ways to make an improvement. The simple act of acknowledging your negative behavior can go a long way toward the interviewer giving you enough of a "benefit of the doubt" to review the rest of your background with an open mind and thus take into account all your professional experiences.

Driving Record A review of an applicant's driving record can be the first indication of the individual's approach toward policies and procedures. This record can also give insight into the applicant's ability to learn from past mistakes. Listening to the applicant discuss driving mistakes also gives an interviewer insight into the applicant's ability to accept or **not** accept responsibility for his actions.

A poor driving record is a red flag that interviewers pay close attention to.

As interviewers review your driving record they will also be looking for the answers to several questions which apply to driving violations:

Speeding: How old was the applicant when tickets were given?

Make no mistake about it: youth is **no** excuse. However, if someone received three speeding tickets before they were 20 years old and they are now 26 with a clean record for six years the interviewer should feel fairly confident that this individual had learned his lesson. In this person's case, ignoring rules and regulations is **not** a **trend**.

On the other hand if an applicant is 30 years old and has received two tickets over the last two years this indicates a possible trend. At 30 this person should be able to control their driving habits. Youthful bursts of disrespect for policies and procedures should be well quelled by this age.

If you are just starting out, dedicate yourself to obeying all driving rules and regulations. (You might end up being late to some appointment but it will be well worth it in the long run.) If you are faced with an upcoming interview and you have some current traffic violations (within the last three years) it is imperative that you accept the responsibility for the tickets. It is a grave error to try to explain why it wasn't your fault:

- I was so tired because I had been working all night,
- It was a rural road and everyone speeds,
- It was a speed trap.

When asked about your traffic violations answer immediately and succinctly:

Interviewer: Do you have any traffic violations in the last ten years?

Applicant: Yes, ma'am. I have received two tickets. One in July, 1997. I was stopped on the highway for going 75 in a 65. The second in December, 1997, was for going 40 in a 30. The officers were correct in stopping me. I paid the fines for each one and have reevaluated my driving habits and dedicated myself to never getting another ticket.

Some interviewers may simply accept this response and move on. Others may not.

Interviewer: Why didn't you "dedicate" yourself to not getting a second ticket?

Applicant: Good question. It was because I thought the first ticket was a fluke. I didn't take it seriously until I received the second ticket.

Or

Interviewer: Why did you get those two tickets in the first place?

Applicant: I am not sure why specifically I was going over the speed limit. I can't say if I was late for an appointment or something. However, it became very clear to me that I was not paying close enough attention to the speed limits.

DUIs: DUIs are a serious matter. The only remedy for a DUI is **time**, a **clean driving record**, and many times, good training records and employment history. Please notice I didn't just say **time**—I said time **and** a clean driving record and perhaps no problems in training or employment.

Once again age may make a difference in the interviewer's outlook. If a 27 year old applicant was charged with a DUI at the age of 19 but has had a completely clean driving record, solid employment history, and no problems in training since this charge, the interviewer could be more inclined to see the DUI as an anomaly, not a trend.

If, however, a 30 year old applicant was charged with a DUI at age 25 and has had several speeding tickets since the DUI an interviewer would be justified in being concerned about a possible trend. The interviewer could well think the applicant is unable, or unwilling, to take responsibility for his behavior and has a lackadaisical approach toward policies and procedures.

An individual who chooses a career as a professional pilot should show maturity at an early age. I become concerned when someone has consistent driving problems over the age of 21.

An addendum to your paperwork for a DUI is important because it allows you to leave your own words with your application packet. In this way, anyone who reviews your packet will have your own words to review, not simply the notes of someone else concerning your situation. Think of this addendum as a way to discuss "in person" your DUI with decision makers you may not meet.

Having said all this you could discover that an interviewer will not accept your addendum. If this is the case, don't push it. You gain a great deal simply by putting down on paper the facts of the DUI. By writing out your explanation you will become more comfortable talking about the matter. This approach of accepting responsibility and being able to discuss it professionally will not go unnoticed. Although it would be nice to leave your written words you still will have made your point in a concise, unemotional manner.

Suspension of license for administrative reasons (uninsured motorist, unpaid parking fines, etc.): I have had clients who have said to me, "My license was suspended because I forgot to renew my insurance. I didn't have an accident or anything, I wasn't speeding, why should the interviewer care?"

A pilot's life and those of his passengers can depend on attention to detail. If someone forgets to renew their car insurance, it's not a huge leap to thinking that the same person might forget to update their airport charts, or their company SOPs, or might forget to do a walkaround. Whether this impression is fair or not is **not** the issue. This is the reality that you, as a professional pilot, must deal with!

Interviewer: Tell me about this suspended license.

Applicant: "Yes, ma'am. My license was suspended because I forgot to renew my car insurance. I did receive the notice to renew. At that time I was short of funds and put the notice away intending to pay it the next month. I then forgot about it. I paid the premium immediately upon receiving the suspension notice. I now make a point of keeping track of the due dates for all my bills."

If your license has been suspended for an administrative problem you must be ready to accept full responsibility for the oversight. Defensiveness on your part will not be viewed positively.

ADDENDUM FOR SUSPENSION OF LICENSE FOR ADMINISTRATIVE REASONS: Yes

ADDENDUM FOR DUI: Yes

ADDENDUM FOR
SPEEDING TICKETS
WITHOUT SUSPENSION
OF LICENSE: No

FAA Records and Airline Training Records

Accident/Incident/ A pilot's record with the FAA is also another
Violation: indication of his approach toward policies,
procedures, as well as his respect for
authority. When interviewing an applicant
with an FAA violation the interviewer will
be reviewing several areas:

- What was the specific reason for the violation?

- Was the pilot violated for breaking the rule unintentionally or intentionally (altitude deviation *vs* buzzing his fraternity house in a 172?)

- Does the applicant show a strong understanding of the value of policies and procedures in other areas of his life?

- Does the applicant accept responsibility for the violation?

For any FAA accident/incident/ violation you should always provide applicable, and concise, documentation which will allow the interviewer to clearly understand the situation.

An addendum will allow you to place your own words in front of the hiring board instead of the notes someone else made about how you presented the situation.

Training Records: A review of a pilot's training records can be extremely telling. An airline wants to hire a pilot who learns quickly and retains information easily. Because checkrides are a constant throughout a pilot's professional life an airline wants to hire someone who begins preparation for checkrides early and comes prepared to shine during testing.

A pilot with a history of failed checkrides, or a constant need for additional training can easily raise concerns about safety, the pilot's motivation toward his career and increased training costs.

There seems to be a slight difference in attitude toward failed checkrides while a student (private, commercial) versus a failure when you are a professional pilot (ATP, upgrade checkride, proficiency check).

If you are just beginning in your career make a promise to yourself to approach each checkride with the professionalism it deserves. Stay up on your studies. Attend study groups offered by your flight school or company.

If you are faced with having to discuss a failed checkride take the time to review why the failure occurred. What, specifically, were the reasons for the failure? Let the interviewer know that all went well until the _____ (fill in the blank!). If you retook the checkride within the next few days with no problems make sure the interviewer is aware of this fact.

One checkride failure doesn't need a written addendum. However, make sure you know the exact reasons for failing the checkride; how much, if any, additional training you required; and when you returned to take the checkride.

Interviewer: Have you ever failed a checkride?

Applicant: Yes, sir. I failed my Instrument checkride. Everything was going well until the missed approach which was the final maneuver. We debriefed the entire checkride. The next day I took an hour of training with my instructor. Five days later I met with the examiner and was only required to complete the missed approach maneuver. I passed with no problems.

If you have multiple checkride failures you might consider writing an addendum explaining the circumstances of each checkride. Keep the explanations succinct.

ADDENDUM FOR FAA ACCIDENT/INCIDENT/VIOLATION: Yes, along with FAA finding letter.

ADDENDUM FOR ONE FAILED CHECKRIDE: No

ADDENDUM FOR MULTIPLE FAILED CHECKRIDES: Yes

Logbooks and Flight Time Paperwork accuracy is of paramount importance in the cockpit. The logbook and flight time calculations are mirrors of a pilot's attention to detail.

Messy Logbooks: It is not unusual for a new pilot to make errors when they first begin keeping a logbook.

As long as the logbooks become neater as the pilot progresses in experience, the early logbooks will usually not be dwelled on.

If you are just starting out, dedicate yourself to assuring that each page of calculations is correct. Remember to always use ink. If you must make a correction **never** use white-out or a cover-up pen (such as black magic-marker) to cover up an entry. Simply draw a line through the error and insert the correction on the first empty line after your last logbook entry.

Be very careful of what you write in the "comments" section of your logbook. These entries will be reviewed by the interviewer! Don't discuss what a jerk your instructor was, or that date you made at the airport.

If your logbooks are consistently messy with lots of mistakes, white-out, etc. you might want to think about rewriting them. Rewriting your logbooks DOES NOT alleviate the need to present the originals! However, what it will do is make it easier for the interviewer to read; it will show that you realize that your logbooks are not up-to-par; and it will give the interviewer the impression that you have done everything possible to make his job easier.

If your logbooks are rewritten, put a statement of that fact in the front page of your new logbook.

This is a duplicate copy of my original logbook. Original logbook available upon request.

REALITY CHECK! *Rewriting your logbooks does not alleviate the requirement of presenting the originals during the interview! Always take your original logbooks to your interview.*

Missing Logbooks: The initial response an interviewer may have to a missing logbook is "What doesn't this person want me to see?"

If you are missing a logbook you absolutely **must** do everything in your power to reconstruct your flight time. Yes, even if you have 6,000 hours and you are missing a logbook that shows your flight time from 200 hours to 600 hours.

Airlines have legalities they must follow. Flight time accuracy is one of these legalities. If you don't reconstruct the time for the interviewer, and they need the information, believe me they will not do the work themselves, they will just move on to the next applicant!

Here are some ideas how to reconstruct flight time:

- Ask your former flight instructors to write a letter confirming when they instructed you and when you took a specific checkride. Ask them to have this letter notarized.

- Review your flight instructor's logbook to see if your name is mentioned when your instructor logged her time during your lesson. Make copies of those pages.

- Gather W-2s from the job you had while flying. This will at least show that you were employed at that company.
- Ask past employers to write a letter concerning the type of aircraft you were flying, and the approximate number of hours you were flying. Make sure they have these letters notarized.
- Gather any flight training records you have for the lost flight time.
- If your logbooks were stolen present the police report.

If you can present at least one, preferably two, of these documents the lost logbook will be less of a problem. If you go in empty handed and expect the interviewers to take you at your word, you could be sorely disappointed.

If you are just starting out make yourself a promise to COPY new logbook pages every month. Invest in a small fireproof safe and store the copies there or use a safety deposit box at a bank.

Overestimation of flight time: Flight time and currency are areas that every airline reviews when deciding to invite a pilot for an interview. Overestimating flight time may mean that you are called in too early for an interview. Put frankly, it is not yet your turn!

We get phone calls every week from pilots who say, "I overestimated my PIC time by [10 to 200] hours on my airline application. Now what do I do?" Well, the only thing you can do is inform the airline of your error. Some airlines will cancel your interview if they discover that your flight time has been listed incorrectly. To help alleviate this situation take the time to do the following:

- Audit your logbooks PRIOR to filling out any applications.
- Fill out each airline application separately!

Each airline has a different way they want flight time to be calculated. Read the directions several times. Have another pilot read the directions and compare your interpretations. If you are confused about how an airline wants flight time calculated, **ask** someone who knows (call the airline, or ask a pilot employee of that airline to research the answer for you.)

Understand that the way the FAA allows you to log flight time and the way the airlines want you to list it on their application can be **very different**. For example, after solo as a student pilot, in your logbook the FAA allows you to log PIC time when flying alone. However, many airlines do **not** want you to add any student time in your PIC column!

- When in doubt, be conservative!
- **Never** anticipate flight time! ("I want to get this application in, I'll be flying 70 hours this month so I'll add that flight time in now." Then you get the flu, are out of flying for two weeks and are now dramatically behind in your flight time.)

- **Never, never** "round up" numbers!

Underestimating Flight Time: Obviously, this is not as serious as overestimating. There is no need to contact the airline prior to your interview.

If you have underestimated be ready to explain why you made this error. Make sure you can clearly explain your correct flight time in your logbooks and on the application.

ADDENDUM FOR MISSING LOGBOOKS: Yes, with time recreated.

ADDENDUM FOR OVERESTIMATION OF FLIGHT TIME: Yes, but, also contact the airline prior to your interview to inform them of the mistake.

ADDENDUM FOR UNDERESTIMATING FLIGHT TIME: No, but be ready to explain your errors.

Past Employment Past performance is an indication of future performance. Your work history is of vital importance to a pilot interviewer. For this reason you should know exactly what each former employer will say about you when a potential employer asks for a reference. (Even though past employers are limited in the information they can provide without the employee's written permission, you never know who will answer the phone on the day that a potential employer calls for a reference.)

Termination from a flying job—Civilian: Being terminated from a flying job is a serious situation. It means that your employer was highly unsatisfied with your performance.

If you were terminated from a flying job it is vitally important that you honestly and completely take responsibility for the behavior that contributed to the termination.

If you have acquired another flying job ask your current employer for a letter of recommendation discussing your positive performance (if he/she knows you are looking for a new job!).

Call the employer who terminated you and find out exactly what is listed in your employment record. You can only truly prepare when you know what you are up against.

If the reason for your termination was your flying it is imperative that you document what you have done to improve (i.e., paid for a type rating on you own; took a flying job that was a "step down" in order to get back in the cockpit and improve your skills, etc.).

REALITY CHECK! If you were given the opportunity to "resign" by your employer don't think the interviewer will be fooled. As a general rule people who are forced to resign have some periods of unemployment, or they take a job that is less desirable than the one they resigned from. These are all red flags to an interviewer.

Suspension from employment—Civilian If you were temporarily suspended from a job it is imperative that you can honestly explain why the suspension occurred. It would also be a good idea, if possible, to get a letter from your employer stating that you have improved in the area that caused the suspension. (For example: you were late several times and were suspended for two weeks without pay. You would want to bring some type of proof that your tardiness is no longer a problem. This proof would be in the form of a letter from your past employer or perhaps a employee critique form that states that your tardiness has been alleviated.)

ADDENDUM FOR TERMINATION OR SUSPENSION OF FLYING JOB: Yes

Military Employment Even without access to military records there are still many red flags that can signal to an interviewer that you may have had problems in your military career. Some of these red flags include:

- Slow (or lack of) promotions due to performance,
- Leaving the military prior to completion of normal duty time,
- Lack of flying for an extended period,
- Changing of aircraft (i.e., jets to cargo).

In addition, it is amazing how much information can be discovered through people just talking! Military aviation is an extra-small world. Don't be misled into thinking that simply because the airlines may not review your military training records that they can't, or won't, become aware of problem areas.

If you have been in front of a military flying board, or were suspended from flying for some reason please do not assume that this information cannot be discovered. We have had several clients who had to resign under an Article 15. Even though their discharge papers said "Honorable," airlines have been able to discover the real reason for the resignation.

NOTE: Many retired military were not promoted simply due to their decision to pursue a civilian career. This is not uncommon and should not be an issue in an interview.

ADDENDUM FOR MILITARY REVIEW BOARD: Yes

ADDENDUM FOR ARTICLE 15: Yes

ADDENDUM FOR LACK OF PROMOTION DUE TO DECISION TO PURSUE CIVILIAN AVIATION: No

Job Hopping— Civilian Having multiple flying jobs is not unusual due to furloughs, bankruptcies, and the continual need to improving one's flying skills.

However, interviewers will be interested in discussing lateral moves or a move to a lesser flying position.

When a pilot makes a lateral move from one job to another this could signal training problems or problems with management. Taking a step 'backward' in your flying (i.e., flying commuter to flying night cargo in a smaller aircraft) can signal the same problems.

When making a job change make sure you have career building reasons for accepting the new job. Such reasons include better equipment, more students (if flight instructing), faster possibility for PIC (if making lateral move).

Reasons for accepting a lower flying position or making multiple lateral moves which may cause concern to an interviewer could be: wanting to move closer to my boyfriend/girlfriend; hated the area of the country I was flying; didn't like the people I worked with.

Your competition is doing everything possible (in many cases enduring hardships such as time away from family) to gain flight time and experience. If your career path shows more interest in being comfortable (flight instructing for five years because you don't want to move even though there were other more experience-building jobs available elsewhere) you will be viewed as less motivated toward your career. This could hurt your chances of being hired. Once again, we are not here to discuss what is right or what is fair. This is a reality of the pilot profession.

ADDENDUM FOR JOB HOPPING: No, but be prepared to discuss the reasons.

Academic Performance   A review of a pilot's grades gives an interviewer excellent insight into the applicant's academic abilities and, to a lesser extent, their motivation to succeed.

If your grades were terrible at the beginning of your college career but steadily improved the interviewer most likely will not be too concerned. An improvement in grades shows an ability to learn from past mistakes.

If your grades were horrible throughout college you should be prepared to discuss why this occurred. In addition you should be able to point out other areas of your life that prove you have strong academic abilities (such as high marks on flight tests, solid checkride history, etc.).

I have had some clients who have gone back to school to take a class or two in order to show the interviewer that they can do the work.

One client had several Fs in math while in college. Even when he retook the math classes he barely passed with a D. Several years out of college, he went back and took Advanced Algebra and Calculus and received an A in both courses. (It wasn't easy he said!) What this did for him in his interviews was alleviate the interviewer's concern about his academic abilities, but it also showed the interviewer that this pilot was motivated to succeed.

ADDENDUM FOR POOR GRADES: No, but be prepared to discuss the reasons for the poor grades.

Unresolved Issues On a regular basis we have clients who are involved in a problem area that has yet to reach its conclusion. Their main question is always, "Should I accept an interview at this time?"

To try to answer this difficult question let's review several different scenarios.

An aircraft accident/incident/ violation that is still being investigated by the FAA: When an applicant has been involved in an investigation with the FAA there are basic questions an interviewer wants answered:

- Was the pilot at fault?
- What type of punishment was enforced?

These questions must be answered before the interviewer can begin answering the follow up questions which include:
- Does the applicant take responsibility?

By the very nature of an ongoing investigation the airline cannot be sure of the answers to the first two questions. Without some conclusion the interviewer is stymied. What if the applicant's license is suspended for six months? What if we hire this person and then discover that this is more serious than initially presented? Because of the uncertainty of the situation it is not uncommon for the outcome of the interview to be negative.

Writing an advice book means having to make generalized statements. Although circumstances may vary, in general, I feel strongly it is not a good idea to be interviewing for a new pilot position with an unresolved FAA investigation.

However, if you make the decision to accept an interview anyway, it is absolutely imperative that you have up-to-date information on the status of the investigation. Request a letter from the authorities that perhaps simply says that the investigation is still ongoing. Present the interviewer with a written statement of what occurred during the accident/incident. Be prepared to discuss what you think happened. You may even be asked what you feel the outcome will be. (You may want to discuss with an aviation attorney the propriety of presenting any verbal or written statement to an outside entity during an ongoing investigation.)

Recent failure in upgrade training: If you fail upgrade training with your current commuter airline or corporate flight department you are faced with presenting an explanation for exactly the type of behavior major airlines are looking to avoid. They do not want to hire pilots who will have trouble becoming a captain, or pilots who show a trend toward needing additional training.

For this reason it is important to resolve the situation before accepting an interview. The easiest solution would be to stay at your company until you can retake the upgrade training. Success after a failure does a great deal to lower the concern of an interviewer.

I had a client who failed his initial upgrade training, twice. This was the first problem he had ever had in training. He was given two weeks off by his company.

During this time he had an interview with a major airline. He was able to postpone his interview for two months.

He took the two weeks off and did nothing but study. He passed his upgrade training with flying colors and was immediately put back on the line. When he went to his interview he was able to show the outcome of his two-week suspension. He was able to prove that his training problem was not the beginning of a trend. He showed that he took responsibility for the failure, took the steps to improve, and was successful. The interviewer discussed the situation with him thoroughly and recommended he be hired.

If you are asked to resign due to lack of upgrade, read on.

Recent flying job termination: Being terminated or asked to resign from a job is, by its definition, a conclusion. But, not the one you want!

If you are terminated, or asked to resign from a flying job, do not spend your time pursuing interviews where the job you are applying for is a step-up from the job you were just terminated from (you were a flight instructor and have an interview with a commuter airline) until you have proven yourself in another flying job!

Let me be blunt: The majority of the time it is futile to try to sell yourself as a commuter pilot when you are coming directly from being fired as a flight instructor. It is usually futile to try to sell yourself as a major airline pilot when you are coming directly from being fired as a commuter pilot. See my point?

The remedy is to get back in the cockpit. You must prove the termination was an anomaly, not a trend.

You may have to accept the same level of flying job from which you were terminated. Perhaps you could be rehired by one of your past aviation employers. You may have to return to flight instructing. Whatever it takes you must have some concrete proof to show the next level employer that you are dedicated to your profession and motivated to improve on a difficult situation. As I stated earlier success after a failure does a great deal to lower the concern of an interviewer.

ADDENDUM FOR UNRESOLVED ISSUES: Yes!!

Less Common Problem Areas

Poor credit Some airlines do credit background checks, others do not.

Even if you feel there is nothing negative listed on your credit history, it's always a good idea to review your credit history on a regular basis anyway because of the unbelievable access companies have to all of our credit history.

When I reviewed my credit history I discovered over 20 companies that had requested information on me (in order to send out promotional offers.)

In addition I discovered that a credit card that I had canceled over a year prior had listed me as a poor credit risk because of a $20.00 late fee. By checking on my credit I was able to challenge this listing and have it removed.

NOTE: The three large credit reporting agencies will send you a form which will stop all selling of your name to these companies for a period of up to one year. See the Do-It-Yourself Background Check information.

ADDENDUM FOR POOR CREDIT: No, and no need to discuss unless asked.

Criminal Convictions Some airlines do criminal background checks, others do not.

If you have a criminal situation in your background it is imperative that you present the information in a logical, honest, and open manner. You will want to bring all applicable documentation including court records, parole reports, etc.

ADDENDUM FOR CRIMINAL CONVICTIONS: Yes.

Notes

CHAPTER 6

Writing An Addendum

An addendum is a written statement describing a problem area or special situation.

An addendum should never go in with your initial application unless the airline requests an in-depth explanation of the problem.

Addendums seem to be appropriate for the following situations:
- Accident/incident/or violation,
- Flying job termination,
- Suspension from your job (i.e., two weeks off for failing an oral or perhaps a month off for poor attitude),
- DUI (driving under influence),

- Suspended driver's license (for whatever reason: DUI, unpaid parking tickets, lapsing of insurance),
- Article 15 from the military,
- Pulled from flying while in the military,
- Subject of a military board,
- Troubled training history (i.e., three or more failed checkrides in your career),
- Suspended from college.

Also Although this is not a problem area in the context of this book you might want to write a short addendum to explain an unusual medical situation. REMEMBER, that any medical information will be discussed during your medical evaluation which will take place after you have received a job offer.

Also If you are missing documentation that the airline requested you bring to your interview (i.e., college transcripts, driving record, etc.) you may want to include a list of what you are missing and why. This will stop their thinking that you simply forgot.

Example:
Missing Documents

John Doe
114 S Nine St.
Dover, NH 03454
1-603-411-811

I requested my Driving Record for the State of Virginia on 2/23/00 and again on 3/10/00. I have not yet received the information. I will forward this information to you as soon as I receive it.

Even though all of these areas will be topics of discussion an addendum is not usually needed for:

- One checkride failure,
- Poor grades in school,
- No college degree,
- Speeding tickets,
- Involuntary separation from the military which was caused by personal choice (i.e., not accepting higher education which is necessary for promotion because you have decided to pursue a civilian aviation career),
- Termination or suspension from a part-time, non-flying, non-aviation job.

An addendum should be offered at the time of the interview. A good way to present it is to place your addendum in with your application. This will allow the interviewer time to read it prior to meeting with you.

Any other documentation (FAA letters, letter from a past employer, etc.) that lends support to the addendum should be attached to the addendum.

Format of an addendum

The addendum should be one page only. It should be typed.

ADDENDUM TO APPLICATION

John Doe
114 S Nine St.
Dover, NH 03454
1-603-411-811
SSN 123-45-6789

[List the area to be discussed)]

Driving Record

[The body of the addendum should be next. The text of the addendum should be factual.]

> *On the afternoon of July 4, 1992 I was stopped by a Maryland State Patrol Officer and given a ticket for driving under the influence.*
>
> *I had been hiking with friends. At around 1:00pm we had lunch. At that time I drank three beers.*
>
> *At approximately 4:00pm we left the park to attend a fireworks display. As I had quit drinking at approximately 2:30pm I was chosen as the driver.*
>
> *We had been driving about twenty minutes when I was pulled over. The police officer initially said the car tail light was out. The officer then noticed that my passengers had been drinking. He asked me if I had been drinking. I answered, "Yes, that I had had a beer about an hour and a half ago." He then asked me to submit to a sobriety test. I agreed and tested over the legal limit.*
>
> *I was taken to the police station, booked, and released. I pleaded guilty to the offense and paid a $200 fine and attended a driving class. I completed the driving class within two weeks.*

The Ending   As a general rule you want to keep emotion or philosophizing out of an addendum and stick to the facts. However, when the mistake you made came directly from a poor judgment call it is acceptable to discuss the lessons you have learned.

This day made a huge impact upon my life. I thought I was safe to drive and I obviously wasn't. I learned that as a pilot I have a responsibility to myself and my profession to make sure the decisions I make are sound and mature. On this day I failed on both accounts. I have rededicated myself to becoming the most knowledgeable, safety-oriented pilot I can be. During my years as a flight instructor I told this story to all my students in hopes they would not make the same mistake.

Since that day in 1992 I have received no traffic violations.

Perhaps you have three failed checkrides:

ADDENDUM TO APPLICATION

Your Name
Address & Phone
Social Security

Checkride History

I failed my initial instrument checkride on 1/9/00. The examiner failed me on the missed approach. I took an hour of additional training with my instructor on 1/11/00. I retook the checkride on 1/15/00 and passed with no problems.

On 7/9/00 I failed the oral portion of my CFI checkride. The failure was based on my teaching explanation concerning a circle to land approach. The examiner felt as though my understanding of the technique was cloudy, thus my explanation would be confusing to a student. I did some additional study of this approach and returned on 7/18/00 to retake the oral. The examiner only required me to explain the circle to land approach. We then went and flew and I passed with no problems.

On 7/15/02, I failed the oral portion of my initial Captain's Upgrade. I was given two days to review the material. I retook the oral on 7/18/02 and passed with no problems.

When The Application Calls For An Explanation

What if the airline application specifically requests an explanation for a problem area but there is little room for long explanations? You want to make sure you list the situation honestly, but without making it sound truly horrible. You may use "application shorthand."

Some examples:
- 3/12/02 FAA Viol.: Medical not avail for ramp ck.. Fine only. Detail avail.
- 2/12/05 Job Term: Refused trip due to legals. Detail avail.
- 4/9/93 DUI. Fine and community srv.

CHAPTER 7

In Conclusion

If you have completed your background search and found everything in order, congratulations!

If you have completed your background search and found an error, congratulations on uncovering it early!

If you have completed your background search and discovered a true problem area in your past (as is the most common situation), congratulations on taking the first steps toward making your mistakes less of an issue!

One of the wonderful things I've discovered about the airline interviewing process is that pilot applicants do have a great deal of control over the outcome of the interview. Nowhere has this proven more true than in the presentation of a problem area.

Openness, honesty, and accepting responsibility for past mistakes go a long way toward lowering the concern level of an interviewer. You can lower it even further if you arrive at your interview with the correct documentation. And, the final icing on the "lowering of concern" cake is being able to prove to an interviewer that the problem area was an anomaly and not a trend.

I have had many clients who have made, what would appear on the surface, to be devastating mistakes in their flying careers. But, through persistence, openness, honesty, and a willingness to change their behavior many clients have achieved their highest career goals!

Index

PRODUCTS AND SERVICES

Cage Consulting, Inc.

Orders, questions, or to set an interview consultation appointment, please call 1-888-899-CAGE or visit our website at www.cageconsulting.com

Books Descriptions and Prices on the ASA website at www.asa2fly.com

Pilot Career Guides

Checklist for Success: A Pilot's Guide to the Successful Airline Interview by Cheryl A. Cage

CHECKLIST Interactive CD: An Interview Simulator. Written and Narrated by Cheryl A. Cage

Airline Pilot Technical Interviews: A Study Guide by Ronald McElroy

Mental Math for Pilots by Ronald McElroy

Reporting Clear? A Pilot's Interview Guide to Background Checks & Presenting Personal History by Cheryl A. Cage

Flight Attendant Guide

Welcome Aboard! Your Career as a Flight Attendant by Becky S. Bock (with Cheryl Cage)

General Title

Your Job Search Partner, A 10-day, step-by-step opportunity producing job search guide by Cheryl Cage (This book is for non-pilots.)

APPENDIX I   *SAMPLE REQUEST LETTER*

Here is a sample letter for use when requesting records or information from various agencies. My instructions are listed in italics. If you cannot type the letters, PRINT CLEARLY!

KEEP COPIES! If you do not receive some information in time for your interview, at least you can prove you requested it!

DATE: *Print the date you are mailing the letter.*

TO: *Fill in blank with agency name, such as:*
                   -National Highway Traffic Safety Admin.
                   -Federal Aviation Administration
                   -Your College Bursar's Office

FROM: *Your name*

REGARDING: *Fill in the blank with your request, such as:*
                   -National Driver Record
                   -Request for Complete Airman File
                   -Request for College Transcripts

Dear Sir or Madam:

I am preparing for an important job interview. For this reason I am writing to request _____ *(list records you are requesting)*.

Here is the information I believe you require to fulfill my request. *(List your personal data.)*
- Full Legal Name
- Return Address
- Social Security Number:
- Date of Birth:
- Contact Numbers: *(List at least two contact numbers in case the agency needs to contact you)*

Then list any additional information that may be required by the specific agency you are writing.

Example

NDR requires the State and number of current driver's license; personal description; letter notarized.
- Current driver's license: Arizona License # 78342
- My description is listed on the copy of my license (enclosed).
- Please note this letter is notarized.
- I understand there is no charge for these records.

Example

FAA requires your airman certificate number (or social security number); your signature; and $10.00 fee.
- Airman's Certificate Number: 555-343-232
- I have enclosed a check for $10.00.
- My signature is listed at the bottom of this letter.

Don't forget to enclose a self-addressed-stamped-envelope if required.

Receipt of these records is extremely important for my interview. I appreciate your help.

Sincerely,

(Sign your name here)

Type your name,
Type your address
Type phone number

On the next page is a completed request letter. Make copies, fill in your information, then mail! If you would like to make the letter larger simply use any copier and expand the size.

DATE:

TO:

FROM:

REGARDING:

Dear Sir or Madam:

I am preparing for an important job interview. For this reason I am requesting the following records/information:

_____

Here is the information I believe you need to fulfill my request:

Legal Name_____

Birthdate_____

Social Security #_____

Street Address _____

City_____State_____ZIP_____

Main Phone_____ Other Phone_____

Additional information you require:

1. _____

2. _____

3. _____

4. _____

Receipt of this information is extremely important for my interview. Your help is greatly appreciated.

Sincerely,

A FINAL NOTE

In any advice book you have to give generalized information and advice. I understand that there are many differences in our individual problems.

If you would like to discuss an area of special concern with me, privately, please call our main office (toll free)
                1-888-899-CAGE
to set an appointment.

I'll do my best to help!

Cheryl A. Cage